Do Nothing

What I Started Noticing After I Set My Status to Away

Jacob Jaffe

Cover design by the author
Edited in collaboration with ChatGPT
ISBN: 979-8-9991732-0-1
First Edition
Published by Fulfilliment, LLC
Bainbridge Island, WA
https://fulfilliment.com/donothing

Printed in the United States of America

For Carolyn, Jonah, and Nora

How patiently you've loved me —
especially when I was tangled up
in what I thought I had to prove.
I haven't solved that.
But I'm getting better.
And I'm learning to offer myself the same grace
you've always given so freely.

CONTENTS

THE BOOK I WOULD'VE SKIPPED

This isn't the kind of book I would've picked up.
I didn't think I needed to.
If someone had handed it to me, I would've shelved it,
ignored it — mocked it as guru garbage.

And I don't have a clean reason why I've written it now.
No big reveal. Maybe it's just where I am —
a way to make peace with some of what got me here.
A way to let it go.

At the time, it just felt normal.
But with some distance, I can see how it built.
Not with a moment. Not with a decision.
Just one choice at a time, with the person I chose early.
Together.

THE LIFE WE CHOSE
I met Carolyn — my wife, my best friend — in high school.
We've been together ever since.

In our twenties, we moved around a lot.
From Seattle to Los Angeles. Boston. Chicago.
There wasn't a roadmap. We just knew we wanted to
build something that was ours.

Not just a relationship — a life.
And we did it together.

Eventually, we came back to Seattle.
She joined Microsoft first.
I followed a couple months later.
And from there, we grew.
Careers. A home. A family.
A plan. A future.

It felt right.
Not perfect by any means — but solid. Honest.

I didn't call it loyalty at the time.
But that's what it was — to Carolyn,
and what we were building together.
It shaped what I said yes to.
And what I didn't stop to examine.

WHAT CAME WITH IT
Our son was born in 2003.
Our daughter arrived three years later.
We were deep into work, parenting, routine.

I don't remember feeling overwhelmed.
I just remember keeping pace — staying in motion.
It felt like the job. The proof.
The way you signaled you were doing it right.

When the opportunity came to move abroad,
we said yes.
First London. Then Tokyo.

It felt exciting, meaningful — like something we'd earned.
A chance to give our kids experiences we never had.
To stretch. To live differently.

But it wasn't reinvention. Just the same rhythm —
exported to new time zones.

The decisions made sense.
The responsibilities felt heavy — but honest.
I wasn't questioning anything.
I'd said yes — and stayed loyal to the version of myself
who kept saying it.
If I sensed anything off, I didn't name it.
There wasn't bandwidth for that.
And even if there had been,
I'm not sure I would've known what to say.

WHAT I TOOK WITH ME
I don't have anything but respect
for the company I worked for.
Microsoft opened so many doors —
for my career, my family,
and for who I had the chance to become along the way.
It challenged me. It rewarded me.
It gave us a life I couldn't have imagined
when I was starting out.
I thrived there.

But I can also see — now — how much of my identity
and energy became wrapped up in producing.
Consistently. Reliably. Without pause.

Do Nothing

The job didn't ask me to lose myself.
But it never encouraged me to hold onto myself either.
Then again, I brought some of that with me.

I don't talk about my dad much in this book.
But this part of me — the need to show up, to be
available, to get it done — came from him.

He was a salesman.
What set him apart, he believed, was his availability.
If someone needed something, he made it happen —
even if it meant being at his desk by 4 a.m.

He never talked about liking the work.
He wouldn't.
Only about getting it done.
About being needed.
About showing up when others didn't.

I didn't learn that through advice.
I learned it by watching.
And I kept defaulting to it long after I stopped noticing.
It became a reflex.
One I didn't see clearly until I got outside it.

That's not an accusation.
Of him. Or of the company.
It's how those patterns start — early, often unspoken,
and hard to see until you're already living them.

Stepping away let me see what I couldn't while I was still
inside it — and that shift is what shaped this book.

WHAT THIS BOOK IS
This isn't a long book. That's intentional.
I have a tendency to overexplain —
in conversation, and in writing.
Caveats, commas, parentheses —
they've been my crutches more than once.
So I tried to write this differently: with restraint,
and without padding it to make it feel bigger than it is.

It's not meant to be a performance.
Just a few honest stories, told plainly.
If they stay with you longer than it takes to read them,
I hope it's because they made something clearer —
not just for me.

PREFACE

Truthfully, I've never been drawn to books that try to tell you how to live.

Me? Writing something like this? It still feels absurd.
But apparently, I'm doing it anyway.

It's not a guidebook.
Not a push for a second act, either.
And it's definitely not a six-pager or a whitepaper —
I'm not here to convince you of anything.

More a slow exhale than a prescription —
it's a record of what surfaced when I finally
stopped managing everything.

At fifty, I had the rare — and fortunate —
chance to finally set work down.

And I'm not here to offer a roadmap.
Just to name a few things I'd missed while I was in it.

I didn't know what I was looking for.
I just knew I couldn't fake my way through another
status update without zoning out halfway through.

In that space, I started paying closer attention —
and familiar rhythms started to feel different.

Do Nothing

This isn't a book about retirement.
It's about what becomes visible
when you stop programming every moment.

I wasn't looking for revelations.
But I stumbled into a few — some humorous,
some humbling — that reframed how I see work, time,
success, and what actually matters.

Fair warning: a few of the stories ahead might sound
more polished than they felt at the time.
Some might even come off as privileged.

I hear that.

I had the resources, timing, and family support to retire
long before most people get the chance.
That part matters — and I won't pretend it doesn't.

But here's what I believe even more:
I didn't need to retire to learn this.
I just needed space.

I wish I'd started noticing those tendencies sooner.
Not so I could've left earlier, but so I could've
lived it differently.

And if you're in the thick of it right now?
That might actually be the best time to start.

I'm sharing this because, if you're at all like I was,
you might be so immersed in the next meeting, metric,
or milestone that what actually needs your attention
barely registers.

Do Nothing

I didn't write this because I figured something out.
I wrote it because — for the first time in a long time —
I began to see things I'd been missing.

And if anything here prompts a shift like that — even
once — *I'm glad I did.*

INTRODUCTION

WITHOUT PURPOSE, ON PURPOSE
This isn't a guidebook.
So I won't start with where I ended up.
I'll start with what everyone asked when I said I was
stepping away from corporate life:
So... what's next?

I had ideas. But I wasn't looking for the next thing —
not a role, not a plan.
After decades of climbing ladders and chasing outcomes,
I didn't want another path. I wanted space.

This wasn't about moving forward —
it was about stepping back.

I started practicing something
I hadn't made room for in years:
trying things out — and letting them go —
without turning every curiosity into a calling or every
pastime into a pitch deck.

So I tried.
For the first time, it felt OK to not know what came next.
It felt strange at first —
like I'd missed a stage everyone else passed through.

Do Nothing

A few things pulled me in: pickleball, side gigs, long walks.
There were family struggles and health scares.
Some days were full. Some days were slow.

And somewhere along the way,
I quietly set my status to *Away*.
Not just on a screen. In how I showed up.

For a long time, I couldn't just explore something.
It had to mean something — or lead somewhere.

It wasn't reinvention. Or optimization. Just the slow
recognition of patterns I hadn't questioned — ones that
shaped how I moved through the day without realizing it.

Now and then, I'll share some of my experiments —
not because they're answers, but because they surfaced
something I hadn't seen before.
That's why they mattered.
They didn't have to work.
Some might inspire. Some won't. That's okay.

I'm still figuring things out — and I hope I always will be.
I won't say that in every chapter.
But I want you to hear it now — because it's true in all of
them, whether I name it or not.

This isn't a book written from the other side
of a big transformation.
I'm still in the middle of it —
and sometimes, I slip backward.

These reflections aren't conclusions — they're snapshots.
Ten of them — each its own chapter.

And if they resonate, it's probably not because I've
landed anywhere — but because I'm still looking.

I'm learning how to stop chasing the next thing.
Figuring out what permission to do nothing really means
— or if I ever believed I had it.
Not to chase a *purpose*. Just to feel what's *full*.
And some days, I do — especially when I remember...
I'm not doing it alone.

—
this part always makes me nervous.
because now it's not just mine anymore.

1 SET STATUS TO AWAY

RECLAIMING YOUR TIME ISN'T AS EASY AS WALKING AWAY
I used to think that once I left corporate life,
my time would finally be mine.
No more urgent emails.
No more packed calendars.
No more chat pings demanding instant replies.
It sounded like freedom.
But it wasn't — not right away.

What I've learned is that walking away from work
doesn't automatically undo the habits work built into me.
I woke up early.
I checked my phone before getting out of bed.
I opened Microsoft Outlook — only now it was pointed at
my personal inbox instead of my corporate one.
And yes, I chased Inbox Zero — like clearing messages
somehow made the day feel accomplished,
even when it wasn't.

It felt productive. Responsible. *Safe.*
But all it really meant was I was handing my time over to
other people's priorities — not my own.
I wasn't working anymore —
but I was acting like I was on the clock.

Do Nothing

No one tells you that stopping doesn't feel like freedom.
After years of running at full speed,
it's more like whiplash.
You have to unlearn it.

I didn't leave because I had a plan. I left because I had
questions I didn't want to ignore anymore.
At the time, I thought those questions were about
what came next.
But they were really about why I'd kept going
the way I had.

It's not as simple as flipping your availability
status to yellow.
Setting yourself to *Away* is a mindset, not a menu option.
It's about giving yourself permission not to respond —
to others, to tasks, and most of all,
to your own restless need to get things done.

And honestly? That kind of permission — to pause,
to disengage — has been harder to learn
than any job I ever had.

This chapter isn't about how I mastered that overnight.
(It didn't come naturally — and I catch myself slipping
back into old tendencies.)
But it's where the real journey started.
I didn't know how to own my time.
And I'm starting to think that's what made it so hard to
know what to do with it.

The Myth of Urgency
Most urgency is self-imposed.
It hit me slowly — like most realizations worth having —
that much of what I once treated as urgent
was mostly fabricated.
For years, I trained myself to respond instantly. Emails,
texts, meeting invites — if it flashed, I was on it.
I thought this made me efficient, reliable, dependable.
What it really made me was always on.
And being always on doesn't make you indispensable —
it just wears you down.

Even after I left, I was checking, reacting, feeling that itch
to prove I was on top of things.
Only now, no one was asking me to.
In those first few days, I checked LinkedIn notifications
like they were stakeholder emails.
I refreshed reaction counts and replied to every
comment like it was going to be part of my next
performance discussion.

What I Didn't Know Was Allowed
I used to hear leaders talk about protecting their time —
blocking out hours for deep work or setting strict
rules for availability.
I admired that.

But I also thought,
That's nice... but people like me don't get to do that.

Except, I could have.
I just didn't.

For most of my career, I equated dedication with
availability. I believed that saying *yes*, responding fast,
and sacrificing personal time would somehow add up —
like I was earning loyalty points I could cash in later.
Here's the truth I didn't understand for a long time:
There's no bonus round for pushing yourself past the
point of being useful.
And pretty much no one is keeping score.

I've come to see that boundaries aren't selfish —
they're necessary.
And while corporate life didn't always make it easy to say
no, I'm pretty sure I could have said it
more often than I did.

It wasn't just people filling my calendar.
It was projects. Priorities. And a deeply ingrained belief
that my value came from relentlessly chasing
opportunities for results.

That instinct to overcommit didn't start at Microsoft.
It started young —
when saying *no* didn't feel like an option.
Saying no felt like gambling with how I'd be seen —
difficult, unreliable, not worth asking next time.
I absorbed that early. And I carried it forward.

Choosing Where (and With Whom) to Show Up

One of the real joys of stepping away
is realizing I get to choose.
Choose which invitations I accept.
Whether that family event, social gathering, or
community project is worth showing up for.
Whether the best use of today is
doing absolutely nothing.

It's funny — I used to pride myself on being the person
who always showed up. The reliable one.
The team player.
Now, I take pride in being selective about where —
and with whom — I engage.
Not because I don't care — but because I care enough to
protect the time I'll never get back.

I try to remember — just because I have time
doesn't mean I'm available.

Letting Go of What People Think

Saying no — or even just waiting to respond —
doesn't come easy when you've spent a lifetime
managing how you're seen.
I don't want to seem difficult or unhelpful.
But I'm learning: how someone receives my boundary
isn't something I get to control.

If I decline an invitation or leave a message unanswered for a day, it's not a reflection of how I value someone — it's a reflection of how I value my time.

And if that's misunderstood?
I've learned not to chase confusion that isn't mine.

Being Caught in the Act

I didn't even realize I was doing it.
While writing this very chapter, I asked my wife, Carolyn, a question — then turned right back to typing before she could even answer.
When I finally looked up, she smiled and said,
"So... do you want to hear what I think?"

That's what being caught in the act looks like.
Not by a manager or a deadline or a calendar ping — but by someone who knows me well enough to see the reflex before I do.

That reflex to keep moving, keep producing, keep responding — even when I've said I want something different. It's still in there.

And honestly, it's helpful.
Because left to my own devices, I might not catch it.
Or I might rationalize it — tell myself it's momentum, or habit, or focus.

But moments like that remind me: I'm learning how to slow down.

Do Nothing

So I try to pause more often before I commit.
To ask, *Is this how I want to spend my time?*
To believe, more and more, that delayed doesn't mean
disengaged — it means intentional.

I started testing it in small ways.
I waited three minutes before replying to a text.
It felt ridiculous — like I was daring myself not to flinch.
But that discomfort taught me something.
So I tried it again the next day.

Now, when I get an invite — whether to a meeting, a
dinner, or a weekend event — I try to ask,
What happens if I say no?

Usually, the answer isn't all that dramatic.
And that helps.

I've even started leaving emails unread overnight —
to see what happens.
(Spoiler alert: the world does not end.)

If those small things feel hard — that's good.
It probably means they matter.

And sometimes, what matters most is being seen —
especially by the people who know when you're not
really there.

WHAT I LEARNED WHEN THE PERFORMING STOPPED
Setting your status to *Away* isn't about disappearing —
it's about showing up.
For yourself.
And for the people who actually matter.
The ones you truly care about.
The ones who truly care about you.

Urgency fades.
Time doesn't come back.
I used to hand it over without a second thought.
To meetings I didn't need to attend.
To people who didn't really need me.
To the idea that being available made me valuable.

Now I try to pause before I say yes.
I feel the pull to prove I'm being useful —
even when no one's asking.
But I'm learning to ask a different question:
Whose time am I giving away right now — and why?

I don't always get it right.
The more I notice, the more I believe: choosing how to
spend my time might be the most honest thing I do.

INTERLUDE

Too early for an interlude? Maybe.
But considering how late I was to most of this,
I figured I'd start making up for it.

YOU WON'T KNOW UNTIL YOU LEAVE
I used to say it myself:
I don't know what I'd do if I left.
Not because I was clinging to work,
but because I'd never really stopped to ask
why I was doing any of it in the first place.

What would I do next? What would fill the hours?
What would feel fulfilling — or at least real?

I thought the hard part would be
deciding what to do after I left.
But the real shift started when I stopped to ask
why I wanted to leave at all.

I worked at Microsoft for a long time, and we'd saved and
prepared — so by the time I was truly ready to consider
retirement, financial stability was no longer the concern.
And once that was settled,
it allowed me to start asking the others.
Should I travel? Volunteer? Consult? Write a book?
Would I miss the pace? The people?

The sense of identity?
Would I be bored? Irrelevant?
What if I left, and then regretted it?

I thought if I just kept turning the questions over, I'd
eventually find the right answer —
and know when it was time.
But I realized I was asking the wrong things.
What I needed wasn't certainty about *what*.
It was conviction about *why*.

That shift didn't solve everything.
But it gave me a place to start.
I stopped seeing retirement as an exit strategy I had to
fully map — and started seeing it as a question I was
willing to live with.

You can imagine. You can plan.
But for me, none of it started to feel real until
I'd actually stepped away — fully.
Not just from work,
but from the reflex to fill every moment.

No more deadlines. No more inboxes.
No more need to justify how I spent my time.

As long as I was still wired to produce,
even enjoying something felt indulgent.
A long walk? A side project? Even nothing at all?
If it didn't feel earned,
it felt like I was misusing the time
I'd supposedly reclaimed.

Do Nothing

But that's the mindset talking — not the truth.
The truth is, stepping away didn't just give me space.
It changed the way I saw that space.

Walk away from what didn't fit — without calling it a
failure. And experiment without consequence —
which, it turns out, was the only real way to start figuring
out what mattered to me.

I'm noticing what fits — and what doesn't.
Some things I tried — volunteering, serving on boards,
picking up paid gigs — were surprisingly rewarding.
Others weren't.

But even that felt like progress.
I wasn't just doing things.
I was paying attention to how they made me feel.
And that's something I never really learned
while I was working.

Fulfillment doesn't announce itself.
It *reveals* itself slowly — if you're paying attention.

What fits today might not fit tomorrow.
And maybe the real freedom is in letting that be true —
without needing a reason to explain.

2 PLAY GAMES

When Free Time Turns Into Court Time

After I stepped away from work,
I thought my calendar would finally breathe.
I imagined looseness. Room to move.
Days that didn't have to take a particular shape.
But I filled it right back up — not with meetings and
deadlines, but with pickleball games
and softball practices.

Turns out, I didn't just walk away from my job.
I brought some of its habits with me.

Funny how, after years of craving open time, I filled it
again — this time with games instead of goals.

At first, it was simple:
Move my body. Get healthier. Meet a few people.
Pickleball felt like my post-corporate version of low-
hanging fruit — easy to join, good for my body,
and way more fun than grinding on a treadmill.
Softball? That was nostalgia, mostly.
A chance to dust off some old skills and feel
part of a team again.

I thought I was passing time.
What I didn't realize was that these games —
just casual hits and friendly matches — would end up
teaching me more about myself, about community, about
competition, and about when to take things seriously...
and when to let them go.

Because whether it's corporate life or a local rec league,
the games we play — and how we play them — tend to
give us away.

I had a lot to learn.

WHEN PERFORMANCE CREEPS INTO PLAY
I picked up pickleball for the exercise, and senior softball
because a local team needed younger players.
Neither was supposed to be more than a way to stay
active, meet a few people, and fill time in a way that felt
healthier than scrolling LinkedIn, wondering what
everyone else was doing with their lives.

But here's what I learned pretty quickly:
No matter how far you think you've stepped away from
your old mindset, competition has a sneaky way of
following you onto the court.

Pickleball hooked me fast — too fast.
It started as fitness — and before long, I was tracking
heart rates and shot percentages like quarterly KPIs —
the kind of performance metrics I thought I'd left behind.

Softball was different — fewer chances to shine,
and way more time to stew.
You stand in the outfield — waiting, thinking, building
pressure around the one or two moments the ball might
finally come your way.

Both taught me things I didn't expect:
How easy it is to turn something you love
into something you measure.
How quickly fun turns into performance —
even when it's just you out there.
And how letting go of winning is often
the only way to actually enjoy playing.

THE CLIMB-THE-COURT WAKE-UP CALL
I was reminded of all this during a recent climb-the-court
event — one of those setups where every win moves you
up, every loss knocks you down, and by the end,
whoever's standing on the top court gets the
bragging rights.

It was supposed to be friendly.
Usually is — until you start caring a little too much about
where you're standing.

I'd been playing well that week — well enough that
when I got invited to join, I felt like I needed to
show I belonged.
Not to anyone else, really... but to myself, and maybe to
the group who'd been watching me play and, in their own
way, were wondering if I could hold my own.

Do Nothing

The night started fine — a few early wins,
a couple of tough points.
But as partners rotated and the competition stiffened, I
found myself slipping into old habits — frustration when
things didn't go right, blame creeping into my thoughts
when paired with a less experienced player.

Somewhere between the self-pity and the scoreboard,
I saw what was happening.

I had two choices: keep spiraling or shift focus.

So I leaned into what I could control — encouragement,
effort, and the reminder that ending the night sweaty and
smiling was supposed to matter more than court position.

We played a few more matches.
The itch to prove something didn't go away.
But I showed up differently — a little looser,
a little lighter.

And yeah, by the end of the night,
I was back on the top court.
We won the final match.

But that wasn't the part I walked away thinking about.
What stayed with me was how easy it is to slip into old
habits — and how different it feels to notice
before they take over.

THE GAME I GOT WRONG

Pickleball wasn't the only thing I turned into a contest.
But with softball, it caught me off guard —
because I didn't expect it.

I thought it'd be fun. Light. A little nostalgia, maybe.
Something to remind me what it felt like to be part of a
team — without all the pressure.
But I showed up carrying pressure anyway.

I hustled in left field, but it wasn't enough to quiet
the noise in my head.
And when I came to bat, I wasn't thinking about fun.
I was thinking: *Don't screw this up.*

What made it harder was realizing
no one else was treating it that way.
My teammates were catching up in the dugout, joking
with friends on the other team.
They were playing for connection — not to perform.

For them, this was the reward.
For me, it felt like something to prove.

And when I noticed that — really noticed —
the game stopped being fun.
I wasn't enjoying the rhythm. I wasn't relaxed. And I
wasn't getting what I wanted — some movement, some
team energy, maybe even a little grass-stained joy.

So I stepped away.
Not because I didn't want to play.
But because I couldn't play the way they could.

WHAT I LEARNED WHEN I LET GO OF THE SCORE
I don't think I've fully unlearned how to perform.
But I'm starting to notice when it shows up —
and why it does.

Even noticing it feels like progress.
Because sometimes, what makes a game meaningful has
nothing to do with winning —
and everything to do with how it felt to play.

3 DO THE HUSTLE

WHEN DELIVERING RESULTS BECOMES A HARD HABIT TO BREAK
When I first stepped away from corporate life,
I didn't plan on hustling.
No side gigs. No passion projects.
No grand entrepreneurial ventures.
I was *done*.

I thought retirement would be all fun and games —
literally. A couple hours of pickleball here, maybe a
softball game there, long walks to fill the gaps.
Active, social, healthy.

But two hours on the court left 22 hours in the day.
And after decades of structuring my time around
projects, deadlines, and deliverables, I realized "free
time" didn't feel free at all —
it felt like a blank I was expected to fill.

It wasn't that I craved busyness — I just wasn't used to
space that didn't produce anything.

So, without really meaning to, I started to fill the space.
Not with work.
With... the hustle.

The Creative Hustle: Print-On-Demand Dreams

It started innocently.

I got curious about print-on-demand businesses —
those online shops where you upload a design, and
everything else like printing and shipping happens
behind the scenes.
It felt like a hobby with just enough
entrepreneurial upside.

I dove in — learning AI tools, designing pickleball-themed
gear, setting up payment systems, and tweaking product
listings for SEO *(because why do something casually?)*

A few weeks later, I had a fully operational storefront —
and exactly zero sales.

And with that, the excitement fizzled.
Not because I failed.
But because I realized I wasn't actually building
something — just keeping busy in a way that
looked like purpose.

The Gig Hustle: Uber & Instacart

Next came Uber.
I figured, *Why not?* A flexible way to stay engaged and
make a little pocket change.

That illusion shattered during my very first ride.

Do Nothing

The app pinged me for a pickup at the local cannabis shop. My passenger stumbled out, stubbed his toe on the curb, and collapsed — launching into a rambling monologue that veered from injury to existential dread.

I spent the ride with one hand on the wheel and the other hovering over the "Help" button, wondering if this was how my post-retirement adventure ended.

He got out. I got five stars.
And I sat there thinking,
What the hell did I just sign up for?

But instead of calling it quits, I doubled down.

I cleaned my truck religiously. Stocked it with water, chargers, and candy. Printed business cards. Built a Facebook page. Added QR codes for direct bookings.

When rides were slow, I picked up Instacart deliveries — quickly learning that hunting down obscure grocery items for minimal pay wasn't exactly fulfilling. Especially when customers weren't available to approve substitutions, leaving me debating whether swapping almond milk for oat milk was a minor adjustment or a crime against humanity.

It wasn't that I hated these gigs.
Some rides were even fun.

But if I'm honest, I wasn't doing them for the stories — or the money.
I think I was chasing the faint relief of being needed again.

Because unstructured time didn't feel free.
It felt like I was flunking retirement.

THE PROFESSIONAL HUSTLE:
PERSONAL ASSISTANT MODE ACTIVATED
After stepping away from Uber and Instacart — first to
care for my mom, then because I realized I wasn't eager
to get back behind the wheel — I shifted into a personal
assistant role for a local property owner.

It was supposed to be light admin work —
9 to 12 hours a week, nothing too demanding.

I even convinced her to let me handle some of it
remotely — something no previous assistant had been
allowed — so I could provide support even while
camping in my trailer.

Because nothing says "enjoying retirement" like
processing invoices and drafting emails surrounded by
pine trees and birdsong.

It didn't take long to realize I was doing the
same thing again.

I was over-delivering on tasks that didn't require it,
polishing processes no one asked to be improved,
and realizing that my experience was being ignored.

Combine that with a paycheck that barely covered gas for
the roundtrip to her "office" — which, in reality, was her
kitchen — and it became clear I needed to move on.

THE COMMUNITY HUSTLE: VOLUNTEERING TO FEEL USEFUL

Of course, not every hustle came with a paycheck.
Some wore the disguise of "giving back."

I joined the Parents Teachers Students Organization
(PTSO) at our daughter's high school — not to organize
bake sales or chaperone dances (both of which I happily
left to others), but to contribute where I could
genuinely add value.

I digitized years of historical records, converted paper
budgets into usable spreadsheets, and overhauled the
website. It felt good — productive in a way that
matched my skills.

But when conversations shifted to how many pies were
needed for Pi Day, I realized I was in the wrong discussion
— not because the work wasn't important, but because it
wasn't where I was most useful.

At the same time, I became Vice President of our
condominium board. Carolyn and I had purchased the
unit so my mom could have a stable, familiar place to live
near us as she aged.

Initially, it felt familiar — budgets, governance,
long-term planning.

What took adjustment was learning that leadership also
meant debating things like how frequently the scuppers
needed cleaning (to be honest, I'm not sure I know what
a scupper does), or exactly when the aroma of a

resident's delicious home-cooked meal crossed the line into an "offensive smell" in shared spaces.

Over time, I stopped focusing solely on tasks and started focusing on people — both on the board and in the broader community.
That shift made the work feel more meaningful —
even when the topics weren't exactly strategic.

I remain on the board today. And while it has its frustrations, I've started to appreciate it differently —
not just for the governance stuff, but for the relationships it's nudged me to build, and the sense of care it's asked me to carry.

I KEPT TRYING
None of these hustles — paid or volunteer —
were really about staying active.
They were about delivering outcomes.

For nearly 30 years, I measured my value by what I delivered — products, plans, decisions.
Stepping into retirement didn't erase that instinct —
it revealed it.

But it did give me something I never had before —
the freedom to stop.

In my old world, starting something and then walking away felt like failure —
like a lack of commitment or follow-through.
Now? I see it differently.

Trying, learning, and deciding *this isn't for me*
isn't quitting — it's control.

It's knowing that just because you can finish something
doesn't make it worth doing so.

If I'd understood that earlier, I might've asked harder
questions — about the projects I signed up for, the
outcomes I felt expected to chase, or the work I kept
doing just because it had already started.

I don't think it takes retirement to see this.

Maybe we all hit moments where we're
just following momentum.
And if we can pause — even briefly — and ask,
Is this still right?
Then maybe we get to choose more often.

Thoughtful stopping isn't weakness.
It's a way of honoring your own time.
I wish I'd practiced that sooner.

WHAT I LEARNED WHILE TRYING TO MATTER
If I could go back and whisper something to
my former self — or anyone still in the grind —
it wouldn't be *don't hustle.*
It would be:

Just because you can deliver something...
doesn't mean you need to.

Do Nothing

Not every skill needs to be applied.
Not every hour needs to result in output.
Not every project deserves to be finished
simply because it was started.

I wish I'd practiced that mindset earlier —
To pause.
To ask, *Is this worth doing?*
And to be okay if the answer was no.

Because if you wait until you "have time" to figure this
out, that time won't feel free.
It'll feel like a test — as if you must prove
it was worth earning.

And before you know it, you'll be running in the same
loops you were trying escape.

Even this — the writing — still tugs at that old urge.
But now I recognize the pull — that itch to produce —
for what it is.

And I choose what to pursue because it fills me,
not just because it fills my day.

That awareness might be the most valuable thing
I can share.

4 TAKE A WALK

NOT EVERY STEP NEEDS TO GET YOU SOMEWHERE
If you'd told me a few years ago that walking would
change anything about how I think, I probably would've
laughed — and accused you of reading too many
mindfulness blogs.

I used to roll my eyes at phrases like *being present* or
embracing stillness — they sounded like corporate fluff,
dressing up basic advice like "take a break" or
"clear your head."
I wasn't buying it.

So when I started walking after retirement,
I wasn't chasing clarity or calm.
I was counting calories.

Pickleball hadn't yet taken over my life, and I wanted
something structured — a way to stay active, explore a
bit, and add a little discipline to my week.

I signed up expecting pleasant exercise.
I wasn't looking to be changed — and probably wouldn't
have trusted it if I felt it creeping in.

THE SLOWEST WAY TO NOWHERE

The guided "discovery walks" were exactly as advertised
— slow-paced strolls with lots of pauses to admire gnome
houses, swap bits of local history, and make sure no one
got left behind.

For someone fresh out of a career built on efficiency,
this was excruciating — in a slow-motion,
small-talk kind of way.
Things hit a low point when a group of friends joined
one of the outings and turned it into a mobile
dinner party recap.
They debated past menus, future wine pairings,
and whether the lamb at that one bistro was actually
worth the hype.

I stood there stewing — half-listening, half-judging —
waiting for the group to move.
But the truth is,
they were getting exactly what they came for.
I was the one treating a nature walk
like a meeting that needed to stay on schedule.
I wasn't ready to slow down yet — so I moved on.

FINDING MY STRIDE — OR SO I THOUGHT

Next, I joined a local walking group with fewer rules.
No guides. No scheduled stops. Just start together,
then find your own pace.

This felt like an upgrade.
But I soon discovered the group wasn't just about walking
— it was about community. Post-walk coffees, gatherings
at members' homes, even annual overnight adventures.
Less fitness club, more social circle.

I respected it — but I wasn't ready for
that kind of closeness.
I'd retired young. Most of the group was older,
already settled into a version of connection
I hadn't caught up to yet.

I often ended up walking beside the same gentleman —
we just fell into step.
Every week, without fail, he'd update me on his
Camino de Santiago prep — always with detailed reports.

"This week I watched a YouTube video on Stage 9 —
there's a tricky incline I'll need to train for."
"I've mapped out my rest days now —
let me tell you about the town I'll be stopping in."

His enthusiasm was genuine —
and I appreciated the consistency.
But over time, I realized he was walking
toward something.
I was just moving — hoping the motion itself
would be enough.

I didn't want an itinerary. Or post-walk lattes.
What I wanted was space.

Do Nothing

So — like I've done more than once when things stop
feeling anonymous — I pivoted.
This time, to solo walks.

FROM SOLO TO STILL CHASING SOMETHING
Of course, I couldn't just walk.
I set OKRs — because even wandering needed objectives.
How far could I go?
How many calories could I burn?
Could I beat last week's distance?

I remember celebrating the first time I hit eight miles.
Not for the view. Not for how it felt.
Just because it looked good on my tracking app.

Walking wasn't downtime. It was performance —
disguised as healthy habit.
It looked like self-care. But it was still a scorecard.

I DIDN'T MEAN TO LET GO
It took a camping trip — and no pickleball —
for things to finally break open a little.
With fewer choices, I defaulted to walking.

But this time, my earbuds were fully charged
and actually worked.
I queued up a podcast — probably nothing more
profound than a bit of sports talk — and set off.

Somewhere along that trail, without meaning to, I let go.
No pace-checking. No mile-counting.

I just drifted — carried by the conversation in my ears
and the movement beneath me.

For the first time, walking didn't feel like a task.
It felt like nothing at all —
and somehow, that was the point.

BACK HOME
These days, my favorite walks aren't solo —
they're with Carolyn and our labradoodle, Guinness.
We rotate between trails, though we have our favorites
— and we're never in a rush.
I still track the activity —
for the big picture, not the benchmarks.
What matters is the walk itself —
and the chance to connect.

Guinness stops frequently — to sniff, to greet other dogs,
and, of course, to poop wherever inspiration strikes.
I used to get frustrated. Now I just pause.
Not because I have to. Because I want to.

These walks are when Carolyn and I really talk.
No screens. No distractions. Just the occasional eagle
overhead or a curious deer crossing our path.

We talk about everything — her work, family updates,
my latest pickleball drama.
And then, now and then, we stumble into the kind of
conversation that reminds me how lucky I am to
walk beside her.

What surprises me is how often I hear myself differently
when I talk to her.
It's not just shared time — it's how we sort things out.

I think back to how I used to walk ahead,
annoyed at the pace.
Now, I move with her. I wait for every Guinness stop,
every friendly dog interaction.

Somewhere along the way, I stopped seeing these walks
as something to complete —
and started wanting them not to end.

WHAT I LEARNED BY SLOWING DOWN
Back in my corporate years, if you'd suggested taking a
walk with no clear destination,
I'd have called it a waste of time.
I didn't understand that unstructured moments —
walking, tinkering, even just sitting still —
weren't indulgent.
They were needed.

Walking became my version.
For someone else, it might be gardening, woodworking —
or just staring out a window for half an hour.
It's not about what the thing is.
It's about letting yourself do it — no proof required.

If I'd realized that sooner, I might've stopped filling every
hour with output — and made more room for wandering,
reflection, or moments that didn't ask for anything back.

Some of the most meaningful steps I've taken were the ones where I stopped needing them to lead anywhere. And if those steps include waiting while your dog finds the perfect place to poop —
That's not wasted time.
That's practice.

Yet there are some things you can practice forever — and still not be ready for.

5 CALL YOUR MOM

I thought about breaking this up —
adding headings, offering structure.
But we never lived it that way.
So I won't write it that way either.

When I think about the phrase *Call Your Mom,*
I feel a mix of emotions.
There's the obvious meaning —
the act of picking up the phone to connect.
But there's also a deeper layer: what does it mean to be a
son? What does it mean to have a mother?

Since my parents divorced when I was around fourteen,
my relationship with my mom got harder —
and stayed that way.
We moved between resentment and
brief moments of understanding.
And we never found steady ground.
And it wasn't until the very end — literally weeks before
she died — that I got a kind of clarity I never expected.

She brought it up herself — though, as usual, not directly.
We were driving back from one of her treatment
appointments — maybe radiation, maybe
immunotherapy — returning to the assisted living facility

Carolyn and I had urgently moved her into.
In the car, out of nowhere, she brought up something I'd
said weeks earlier: that I thought she hated me.

She didn't deny it.
Instead, she gave me what she framed as an explanation.

When my parents divorced, I had been asked which
parent I wanted to live with.
I chose my dad. I even remember saying,
because I didn't want him to be alone.
And although my choice was made out of compassion,
my mom took it as a betrayal.
From that moment forward — though she never said it
until that drive, decades later — she harbored intense
hurt, resentment, and yes, hatred toward me.

I screamed.
From somewhere deep — raw, unplanned.
"Are you fucking kidding me?!?!"
I cried.
I swore.
I asked how she could have made me choose, punished
me for it, and then carried that grudge for forty years.
I told her she was awful.
That she should be ashamed.
And I grew even more frustrated that she chose to drop
this bomb at the end of our time together —
a long habit of hers, manipulating situations to extract
more time, more attention, more guilt.
I told her I needed to stop talking
before I said something truly dangerous.

Do Nothing

I don't remember exactly what happened next.
But I do remember this:
Before I left her that day — before I could stop myself —
I said,
"I forgive you."
The words came fast. Too fast.
I wasn't sure if I meant them.
But I didn't take them back.
And that uncertainty sat with me
longer than the anger did.

My first reaction was confusion.
Why did I just say that?
I didn't feel lighter. I felt angry. But over time,
something settled.
It wasn't about me.
Her pain, her resentment — they were hers.
Not for me to fix.
Not for me to carry.

In her final days,
when she said she loved me, it rang hollow.
But it no longer mattered.
I had said what I needed to say.
I had done what I needed to do.

If you rewind the story even further — back to my
childhood — you can see the patterns long before I
understood them.

Some of my fondest memories are from Saturdays
in downtown Seattle.

My mom and I would meet my grandmother
at the doorman of a fashionable department store
in the heart of the city.
I can picture the lobby:
grand, hushed, almost cathedral-like.
The doorman stood there in full uniform,
dignified and imposing.
As a small kid, I felt tiny walking into that space, like the
world had suddenly become very formal and very big.

We'd say hello, exchange hugs,
and head down to the basement diner for lunch.
I can see the diner stools and feel the excitement of
spinning on them in endless loops.
And I can hear my grandmother, after taking the first sip
of her steaming chicken and rice soup, squinting at me
with a sly smile and saying:
"Piping hot."

After lunch, the magic would fade.
It was time for daycare.
Yes, even when I was almost certainly far too old for it,
I'd be dropped off at what I remember as the seventh
floor, where the store offered a daycare service.
There I'd build endless structures with Brio blocks while
my mom and grandmother enjoyed "grown-up" shopping
time without me.

I felt out of place there. Too big for the toys.
Too old to be corralled like that.

Old enough to notice the way the attendants' smiles felt
thinner when they looked at me,
as if even they weren't quite sure why I was there.

Later, we'd regroup for dinner — sometimes at a
wonderfully Americanized Chinese restaurant named
Louie's — and for a moment,
the day would feel warm again.

But then came the car ride home.
Without fail, my mom would recount all the ways
I had embarrassed her.
Every misstep.
Every perceived slight.
Every moment she thought reflected poorly on her.
Even the happiest days weren't just happy.
They were a rollercoaster: brief joy, then inevitable pain.

My mom, on the surface,
was everything you'd want her to be:
The Energizer Bunny.
The consummate hostess.
The brightest smile in the room.
She asked questions.
Made you feel heard — even if her profound hearing loss
meant she rarely caught what you actually said.
She was a gatherer of information,
a trader of gossip, a connector of people.
She loved fiercely — but only on her terms.
Only when it suited her image.

And if you scratched just below the surface,
you'd find something very different.

Do Nothing

Especially if you were close enough — like a son —
to see the real version.

As I grew older, I realized I wasn't
chasing her love anymore.
I was chasing her acceptance — validation.
It's funny — while driving away from those downtown
lunches, I wasn't hoping to hear,
"You were the most polite, wonderful boy today."
But maybe I was.
I never heard that.
Not really.

Instead, my relationship with her
was a constant recalibration:
Maybe if I achieved more.
Succeeded more.
Helped her more.
Maybe then.

After the car ride confession — when she admitted the
grudge she had harbored for decades —
our relationship changed.
Not in a way that brought us closer or repaired anything.
But in a way that made it less strained.

I stopped trying.
I stopped chasing.
I didn't need to prove anything anymore —
not to her, and not to myself.
When she said something ridiculous, I just smiled.
When she fumbled with technology, I helped —
more patiently than before.

Do Nothing

I didn't correct her anymore.
I didn't try to change her.
She was who she was.
And for the first time, I let that be true.

As the end approached, I tried one more thing.

My mom and my sister hadn't been in much contact for
close to two years. There was a long, tangled history
between them — and honestly,
between each of them and me.
I had understood from my mom that my sister had been
financially dependent on her well into mid-adulthood,
and seemed to create a cycle of negativity that neither of
them ever really broke.
Over the years, my sister's made a lot of choices
I question — and some of my mom's more difficult traits
show up in her, too.
It's probably part of why I haven't had a relationship with
her in a long time.

But I knew the pain my mom carried
from that estrangement.
And even though I'd done everything I could to avoid
being pulled into their dynamic, I thought that maybe —
just this once, at the end — there might be a window to
make something small whole.

So I reached out.
Not to broker peace.
Not to solve anything.
Only to make it possible.

Do Nothing

My sister did end up coming to visit.
I didn't ask a lot of questions.
I didn't want to know the details.
I'd long stopped talking to my mom about my sister —
those conversations always turned tense, and my only
boundary was that I didn't want to be dragged back in.

But I had the sense my mom got something
from the visit.
Maybe not resolution, but something.
And that was enough.

Later, after my mom was gone, I passed along a final
invitation to my sister — a chance to join us as we
released my mom's ashes, if she wanted.
I didn't have to, but I did.
She thanked me but didn't say whether she'd come.
She didn't.
I had offered what I could.
And that was enough.

When my mom died — about an hour after I left her side
one afternoon — I cried.
Not right away.
At first, it was just logistics: the call from the facility,
the confirmation, the matter-of-factness of it all.
But as I drove away in silence, the emotion finally came
— not in a flood, but in a hollow release.
More than sadness — it was the weight of finality.

Do Nothing

That day, I had sat with her for hours, playing Elvis songs.
She'd long been a super-fan, and a few weeks earlier —
on one of our drives back from treatment — she told me
that "If I Can Dream" was her favorite.
I put it on repeat.
I told her to put on her dancing shoes —
a nod to the stories her own mother used to tell her.
I told her it was okay to let go.
That it was okay to find peace.
By then, she was unresponsive.
But she listened, I think.
Maybe she even heard me.
And that was enough.

It's been about a year since her death.
Just a few weeks ago, my family and I dropped her ashes,
inside a biodegradable container, into the waters along
the route taken by the ferry boat that carries cars and
passengers to and from Seattle — a ride she'd grown
fond of during her final years living near us.

A lake east of Seattle had been her childhood Shangri-La
— a place of calm and joy she returned to in memory.
She chose the water as her final resting place,
because it brought her a version of that peace.

When the container touched the waves, I was struck by
the distinct "thump" it made — a surprisingly loud sound
for someone so demure, so physically small.
She was barely 4'10", if that.
But in that moment, it didn't feel small at all.

Do Nothing

As we stood on the deck, the ferry's horn blew once.
Then again.
By the third sounding, I could no longer
hold back the emotion.

It wasn't only grief for losing her — it was for what my
mom had already missed, and what she would never see:
Our daughter's high school graduation, just weeks away.
The Alaska cruise she booked with our daughter,
a graduation gift.
The Las Vegas trip she planned for our son —
because in her mind, giving to one meant giving to both.
The smaller moments.
Stories she won't hear.
Questions she won't ask.
Quiet pride she'll never get to feel.

It was a good day.
Even beautiful.
The weather cooperated.
My family was by my side.
But beneath it all, there was a deeper hollowness.
Not everything had been healed.
Not everything had been said.
The real losses had happened long ago.
Her passing didn't erase them.
It just made them permanent.

Do Nothing

I didn't set out to heal some great wound
with my mother.
And I didn't.
But now I can see the deeper lesson:
I spent years trying to earn
what my mother never offered.

What set me free wasn't finally getting it.
It was realizing I didn't need it.
And forgiving her — and myself —
for the invisible contracts we lived under.
Ones no one ever agreed to.

6 CHECK YA HEAD

How I Found Out There Was a Tumor in Mine
They say caring for others teaches you
how to care for yourself.
I'm not sure that's true.
At least, it wasn't for me.

In the months after my mom's passing, I thought I was
finally finding my footing again.
And then — almost exactly a year later — I found myself
back in another hard place.
Only this time, it wasn't someone else
I was worried about.
It was me.

For most of my working life,
I didn't think a lot about my health.
I mean, I thought about it, in the way someone thinks
about flossing or stretching —
aspirationally, vaguely, and only when something hurt.
I think I took better care of our cars
than I did my own body.
And maybe because of that, I'd had some stuff:
repeated bouts of gout, Bell's palsy, shingles,
stress-related this-and-that.

Was it depression causing my malaise, or just fatigue?
Who could tell?

The truth is, when you're working full time —
especially in high-pressure environments — you can
convince yourself that almost anything is manageable,
or at least ignorable.
Time is short, stress is high,
and every ailment can be explained away by the job.
But retirement removes the job.
And with it, the excuses.

Suddenly, I had time.
Time to walk. Time to play pickleball. Time to eat better.
Time to "get healthy."

But what I hadn't realized was that giving yourself time to
get healthy also gives your body time to speak up.
And mine had a lot to say.

IT STARTED IN VANCOUVER
Carolyn and I were doing one of our now-traditional
one-night repositioning cruises from Seattle to
Vancouver, British Columbia — a quirky little annual trip
we've come to enjoy these past few years.
This time, we tacked on a few extra days in Vancouver,
a city we've both loved visiting since our
high school days.
It's world-class, cosmopolitan, nostalgic.
We were feeling good.

Then the pain started.
Behind my left eye.
Sharp, like an ice cream headache — only louder.
I'd had headaches like this before,
but not for at least a year.
This one came at roughly the same time each day,
lasted an hour or so, and left me wiped.
Occasionally I could manage it with ibuprofen,
but only barely.
On the second or third day, it was bad enough I had to lie
down in the middle of the afternoon —
something I almost never do, especially on vacation.

I had also been noticing strange visual symptoms:
light trails, little flashes, a weird sensation like my left eye
was lagging behind my right.
The kind of thing you can't quite explain
but you know isn't normal.

By the time we got home,
the headaches had mostly stopped.
But the visual weirdness — which had actually started
well before the trip — lingered.
So, reluctantly, I called the nurse line.
They recommended urgent care.

Urgent care was... fine.
They ran the usual checks, asked the usual questions.
The headaches had resolved,
but the vision issues were vague — hard to pin down.

Do Nothing

I walked away with a "probable migraine"
and an "unlikely to be anything serious" verdict,
along with a couple of prescriptions I never took.
They told me to follow up with
primary care and optometry.

I did — and honestly felt like I'd just wasted everyone's
time, including my own.

My primary care doc, as usual,
was thoughtful and supportive.
We talked through what it probably was — or wasn't —
and he agreed the symptoms didn't raise major red flags.
But he heard me out when I said I wanted to
rule out anything serious.
He suggested a CT scan;
I asked if that would be detailed enough.
He admitted an MRI would be better and placed the
referral — just not urgently.

Around the same time, I also went in for
the optometry appointment.
I tried to explain the visual strangeness,
but it ended up being a standard glasses check.
I walked out with a new prescription and a trip to Costco
for updated progressive lenses, hoping my symptoms
were nothing more than outdated eyewear.

THE SCAN THAT CHANGED EVERYTHING

I delayed the MRI.
Not because I wasn't concerned — I was.
But I'd planned a trip to Puerto Vallarta,
including a family vacation with our kids,
and I didn't want bad news to ruin it.
I needed that time.
I didn't want to be looking at beach sunsets wondering if
they were the last ones I'd see.
So I booked the scan for early January,
after we were back.

The scan was at a facility about an hour from home.
Down in the basement.
Quiet. Cold.
When they came to get me, we walked outside
into the chilly gray mist typical of January days in the
Pacific Northwest and stood on the metal platform that
slowly raised me up to the entrance of the enclosed
trailer that housed the MRI equipment and operator.

I changed into the oversized paper underwear and
unflattering gown, handed over my watch and wedding
ring, put on the multiple levels of ear protection, and got
on the table.
The machine started up.
I felt oddly calm.
Fifteen or so minutes passed.
Then came the curveball: they asked to place an IV
and run a second round with contrast.

That wasn't part of the original plan.
And I knew — I knew —
that meant they found something.

My heart dropped.
Not in some poetic way — it just sank.
I said yes.
I held still.
I got through it.
But I walked out knowing something was in there.
I just didn't know what.

The Worst Phone Call of My Life

That was a Thursday.
Friday morning, the phone buzzed early.
"Hi, is this Jacob?"
"Yes."
"Can you confirm your date of birth?
I'm calling with a referral..."
I asked, "A referral for what?"
What I heard — what I thought I heard — was oncologist.
I shot out of bed.
Panicked.
Certain I was going to die.

My thoughts spiraled instantly: Carolyn would be alone.
Our kids would be fatherless.
I was sure this was it.
I barely heard anything else the nurse said.
My body was shaking.

I started to cry.
I felt like I was going to puke.

Only later, when Carolyn calmly asked the nurse to
repeat herself on speakerphone,
did we hear the actual word: endocrinologist.
Not oncologist.
Not cancer.
Not exactly relief.
But it slowed the spiral.
And that was enough.

THE DIAGNOSIS: ON AN APP, NOT IN PERSON
After the call, I checked my phone.
A message had already hit my patient portal.
My primary care doc had written:
"Your MRI is back and it shows a mass in the area of the
pituitary gland that is likely causing the vision changes...
I've placed a referral to neurosurgery,
endocrinology, and ophthalmology..."

And below that, the radiology report:
Sellar mass. Left cavernous sinus invasion.
Vascular encasement. Pituitary macroadenoma.
I didn't even know what half those words meant.
But I knew enough to be scared.
I looked them up.

My endocrinology appointment was set for four days
later, and that time in between was brutal.
I cried — often.

Do Nothing

Sometimes without warning, sometimes in full collapse.
I'd be fine one moment and folded the next.

Carolyn was steady, as always, but I could feel the fear
just beneath her surface — in the way she reached for
my hand more often, in the things she didn't say.
We even talked about the things we'd tried not to say out
loud — the "what if" scenarios.
What if I died.
What if this was the thing that took me out.
We didn't dwell there, but we didn't avoid it either.

We reviewed our financial accounts.
Made sure she had access to my logins and the code to
the safe where our legal documents are stored.
I walked her through the furnace maintenance schedule
and when the gutters usually needed cleaning.
We discussed the name of the propane guy.

It was awful.
And it was oddly specific.
The kind of clarity that shows up not just in the big stuff,
but in the small, almost ridiculous details.
Like my dying might be manageable — as long as she
remembered who to call when the tank ran low.

Those four days stretched on endlessly.
Time didn't move — it warped.
Every quiet hour opened more room
to imagine the worst.
And I excelled at filling that space.

By the time we left for the endocrinology appointment —
nearly two hours away — I didn't know what kind of
future I was heading toward.
I just hoped I had one.
And I was scared I wouldn't.

THE FIRST REAL CALM
She was phenomenal.
Knowledgeable. Steady. Human.
Also — intense.
The kind of intense that exudes confidence
but makes it hard to get a word in edgewise.

We drank from the firehose.
She was full of information.
But the depth of her explanation helped paint a fuller
picture — not just of the tumor, but of what to expect,
what to watch for, what came next.
As an endocrinologist, she'd seen cases like mine.

She didn't call it a prolactinoma yet — that came later —
but she explained what a pituitary macroadenoma was,
why mine was causing the symptoms I'd described,
and how we'd move forward.
She listened to Carolyn's questions,
including the most important one:
"Will he die from this?"
"No."

That answer changed everything.
It didn't end the fear, but it reframed it.
For the first time, I felt like maybe — just maybe —
I wasn't in free fall.

SYSTEMS SPUTTERING

A couple days later, I drove an hour for what was
supposed to be an ophthalmology appointment.
A few days before, they called to say I'd be seeing
optometry instead — "how it works," they said.
They'd evaluate me first and refer up if needed.

I was already uneasy.
My referral was for something "better,"
and this felt like a downgrade.
I didn't want layers.
I wanted expertise and quick answers.

When I arrived, it got worse.
The whole reason I was there — the visual field test —
almost didn't happen.
It wasn't listed in the appointment notes, and the one
person trained to run it was already backed up.
I had to push for it. Again.
And I was furious.

After all this, how was I the one juggling everything —
making the calls, tracking the steps,
pushing the system forward?
They ran the test.
My visual field was intact.

That was good news.
But the whole experience just confirmed
what I already knew:
I was the project manager of my own survival.

At work, I wasn't someone who avoided responsibility.
I delegated. I supported my team. I made things happen.
But when it came to advocating up — for myself,
for my own growth, for the things I actually wanted —
I hesitated.
I held back.

The clearest example?
My Chief of Staff role.
I loved that job.
I wanted to stay in that job.

But there were two widely accepted beliefs — not mine,
but part of the company culture — that boxed me in.
First, that staying in a "staff" role beyond three years was
career-limiting — a signal to others that you lacked
ambition or couldn't handle a more "real" role.
And second, that I was already at the ceiling for the job.
Too senior to stay. Not eligible to grow.

I pushed, a little.
I made the case.
I was told I was ready for promotion —
just not in that role.
I saw external candidates with less experience,
and certainly less internal knowledge, hired at levels
equal to or above mine.
But I didn't push harder.

Do Nothing

I didn't leave.
I called it loyalty, but maybe it was really about safety.
Or inertia.

What I see now — what I wish I'd understood then —
is that staying quiet doesn't protect you.
It just delays the cost.

You think you're preserving relationships,
credibility, options.
But you're really giving away ground
that's hard to get back.
And the longer you stay quiet,
the harder it becomes to speak at all.

Part of it was the system.
Part of it was timing.
But part of it was me.

I knew how to manage.
I knew how to advocate.
I just didn't always apply that to myself
when it counted most.

And in a way, that's part of what the tumor exposed.
That I'd been tuning out my own signals for a long time.
I didn't check in.
I didn't ask.
I didn't believe that speaking up for myself — in the
moments that mattered most — was allowed.

The symptoms got my attention.
But the wiring underneath — the patterns I'd carried for
decades — that's what really needed looking at.

Finally, a Name

It took another ten days, but Carolyn and I finally made it
to the neurology appointment — a ferry boat across the
water to Seattle, then an Uber from the downtown dock,
tension riding with us the whole way.

The January wind had stirred up waves —
not dramatic, just unsettled.
The kind that make the boat pitch a little,
just enough to feel it in your stomach.
Just enough to remind you what's moving underneath,
even when the surface looks still.

It felt familiar.
That's what the last few weeks had been: waves.
Hope, then fear.
Clarity, then uncertainty.
Some days I felt calm.
Other days, I felt like I was drowning in questions
I didn't know how to ask.

I'd already been told the tumor was likely benign.
But part of me believed the neurosurgeon
might say otherwise.
That the size, or the proximity to my carotid artery,
meant surgery was urgent — or worse,
that it wasn't even possible.

My radiology report had used the word encased.
That word stayed with me.

He was excellent.
Calm. Thoughtful. Straight-shooting.
He named it: prolactinoma.
A benign — but intrusive — pituitary tumor.
Treatable, often very successfully,
with a dopamine agonist.
No surgery needed. At least for now.

He told us about a friend who'd had the same thing —
treated with medication.
It worked. Almost too well.
The tumor shrank so quickly that spinal fluid began
leaking through the sinus wall.
He described the taste, the urgency, the need to go
straight to the ER if it ever happened.

It was oddly comforting.
Not because it made things feel safe,
but because it made them feel known.
Named. Tracked. Watchable.

He ordered a CT scan —
just in case surgery became necessary.
He referred me for another MRI in four months,
and scheduled a follow-up to talk then.
He walked Carolyn through what to watch for:
stroke-like symptoms, severe disorientation, the kind of
headache that earns the phrase "worst of your life."

His overall prognosis was positive.
Yet, there was no illusion that I was in the clear.
Just that we had a plan.
And a way to know if it wasn't working.

SHIFTING GEARS

That's where I am now.
I've started treatment.
I've had follow-up scans.
I'm not cured.
But I'm no longer afraid this will kill me.

I haven't felt many side effects — maybe none.
In most ways, life feels normal.
I take pills twice a week.
I go to my appointments.
I get my labs drawn.
There's a rhythm to it now.
But it never fully fades into the background.
It's always there, somewhere underneath.

And somewhere along the way, I realized that how I
handled all of this — tracking symptoms, organizing care,
managing specialists and appointments across five cities
(some more than once) — wasn't all that different
from how I worked.
A task to complete.
A problem to solve.
Resources to coordinate.

I didn't want to be back in project mode.
But apparently, even when you retire,
some parts of you don't.

That realization sat uncomfortably.
I thought I'd left all that behind — the scheduling,
the control, the instinct to over-function.
But here it was again, keeping me upright.
And maybe that's the tension I'll never fully resolve:
learning to let go of the systems I once built my identity
around, while relying on them when it matters most.

HOLDING THE EDGES
At first, it made sense.
We didn't want to scare our kids.
We didn't want to create worry before we had answers.
Carolyn knew. And for a while,
that felt like the right choice.

Even after the diagnosis — even after we had a name for
it, a plan for treatment, a prognosis that was more
reassuring than terrifying — I didn't say much.
Beyond our kids, I told just one friend.
Carolyn shared it with a few others,
and I appreciated that.
But I didn't reach out or invite others in.

I said it was because I felt fine.
Because it wasn't urgent.
Because it wasn't a big deal.
And maybe some of that was true.
But the deeper truth is harder to name.

I've always filtered.
Not just what I share — but how I say it.

Do Nothing

I soften the sharp edges.
I add caveats, disclaimers, clarifications.
I try to shape the emotional impact
before the words ever leave my mouth.

It's not dishonesty.
It's habit.
Control, maybe.
Or consideration.
Or both.

And if I'm honest, part of it was fear.
Not just of worry, but of being judged —
as broken, or weak,
or somehow exceptionally flawed.
And this thing — this tumor — didn't fit the usual script.

Even as a former product marketer,
I didn't know how to frame it.
I didn't know how much space
it was supposed to take up.
So I shrunk it down to a sentence.
Or said nothing at all.

And maybe that keeps things manageable.
But it also keeps people distant.

Sometimes, the harder thing isn't being vulnerable —
it's letting go of the need to manage
how your vulnerability lands.
I understand that now.
But the instinct to shape how I'm perceived still lingers.

CHECKING MORE THAN JUST THE SCAN
It turns out Check Ya Head isn't just medical advice.
Yes, something was physically wrong — but there was
also something I hadn't been honest about emotionally.
I was wired for stress.
My system ran on it.

And when the symptoms hit,
I didn't just question my body.
I questioned everything.
Am I overreacting?
Am I weak for being scared?
Am I making a big deal out of something small —
or worse,
a small deal out of something big?

That's what no one tells you about health scares.
They don't just shake your body —
they rattle your confidence.
Your judgment. Your sense of what's real.
And the scariest part?
I didn't fully trust myself anymore.

WHEN THE HEAD IS QUIETLY OFF
It wasn't just the tumor.

I've never been diagnosed with anything related to
mental health — and maybe that's not an accident.
I didn't want a label.
I didn't want to explain myself.

Do Nothing

But if I look back honestly, the signs were there.
Long stretches where I felt off.
Flat.
Disconnected.
Like I was moving through my life
with the sound turned down.

The effort it took to fake enthusiasm —
to project confidence, to keep chasing impact —
it started to wear thin.
And eventually, it just stopped feeling worth it.

That's not the same thing as giving up.
It's just... not joy.
Not meaning.
And definitely not health.

Then you add a tumor quietly disrupting hormone levels,
and it becomes harder to pretend
it was all just circumstantial.
Something had been misaligned for a while —
chemically, emotionally, mentally.

Checking ya head isn't just about scans and symptoms.
It's about learning to hear yourself again.
Because when you get used to muting discomfort,
even your own warning signs
can start sounding like background noise.

WHAT I LEARNED WHEN I FINALLY CHECKED IN
If I've learned anything,
it's that ignoring my body didn't make it quieter.
It forced it to get louder.

This chapter isn't really about brain tumors
or MRI trailers or scheduling mishaps.
It's about what happens when you finally have the space
to listen — and realize you don't know how anymore.
Or worse, that you've stopped believing what you hear.

For most of my working life, I filtered everything —
pain, fear, fatigue, even joy.
I managed how I felt.
I managed how I was seen.
I managed other people's comfort
before I considered my own.

I didn't ignore my health, exactly.
I just treated it like background noise —
always there, always explainable.
Stress. Age. Busy.
Whatever excuse fit the calendar.

And I believed, for a long time,
that resilience meant not needing anything.
Especially not help.

I can see how long I'd been off —
emotionally, physically, hormonally —
and how little permission I gave myself to ask why.
Or even consider stopping.

Do Nothing

So what do I wish I'd done differently?

I wish I'd treated check-ins like real work.
I wish I'd used the systems I was so good at building —
schedules, plans, follow-ups — to support myself,
not just everyone else.
I wish I'd stopped mistaking numbness for strength.
Most of all, I wish I'd understood sooner that rest isn't
something you earn by being useful — it's what lets you
hear what's real before it has to start shouting.

Retirement didn't make me sick.
It just made it impossible to pretend I was fine.

7 TALK TO STRANGERS

WHEN CONNECTION COMES FROM THE UNEXPECTED
When I got the diagnosis, I told just one person.
Outside of Carolyn, that is.

It wasn't because I didn't have other people in my life.
Or that I wanted to keep it secret. I just...
couldn't imagine having to reassure someone else
while I was falling apart.

I asked first — "Is it okay if I share something personal?"
— and when he said yes, I told him. He listened.
He didn't flinch, didn't freeze, didn't ask invasive
follow-ups or pivot into a story about his cousin's tumor
or his own medical trauma. He just held it.
Then he said thank you. Not for the story — for the trust.

He didn't try to fix it. He didn't interpret it.
He didn't offer advice.

And weeks later, without prompting, he checked in.
One line, no pressure. Just: "How are you doing?"

He didn't seem to feel like he had to keep tabs or get the
latest update. He wasn't trying to stay informed — he
was trying to stay connected. There's a difference.

I don't know if that counts as being a good friend.
But I know how it felt.

It felt like I didn't have to take care of him
while telling the hardest story of my year.

It didn't fix anything. But it made the fear feel less lonely.

What Even Is a Friend?

I didn't grow up with a definition of friendship that made
sense to me. But I definitely inherited one.

My mom was always asking about my social life.
Not in a casual, *How was your day?* kind of way.
More like an ongoing audit. Who did I hang out with?
Who had I seen lately? Who was coming over?
What was I doing with them?

There was a tone underneath it all — a pressure,
sometimes silent, sometimes not — that friendships were
something you were supposed to collect and prove.

I don't remember her asking much about what I was
thinking. What I believed. What I was building toward.
But if I had plans with someone,
that was "proof" I was doing alright.

Even now, when I use the word *friend*,
I feel it carrying weight.
Like it comes with a subscription fee.
Are we in regular contact? Have we gone deep enough?
Do we text back fast enough to qualify?

Do Nothing

But here's the truth:

The people I value most today don't require any of that.

They don't measure connection in check-ins.

They don't keep track of who texted last.

They don't confuse availability with affection.

They're curious. They're kind.
They don't need to agree with me to support me.

And they don't need to be in touch constantly to feel real.

And maybe that's the shift:

Not just who I call a friend — but what I think
I need a friend to be.

At work, we had names for everyone:
colleague, partner, associate, direct report.
The labels told us how we were supposed to relate.

In life, we tend to do the same.
But the older I get, the more I think those definitions
might be holding us back.

What if the kind of connection that fills us up isn't the
one we maintain forever, but the one that meets us
honestly in a moment?

What if we've been holding on to people out of
vocabulary, not vitality?

WHEN BEING RELATED ISN'T THE SAME AS BEING SAFE
There are a lot of people I'm related to who I no longer
speak with. That's not something I say proudly.
It's also not something I say with regret. It's just... true.

Over time — and often without drama — I've quietly let
go of most of my extended family. Some of it happened
gradually. Some of it came after a few unmistakable
moments. But none of it came from a blow-up or a formal
goodbye. I just stopped showing up for relationships that
made me feel like an NPC — a background character —
in my own life.

I remember being at family gatherings as a kid —
holiday parties, birthdays — and listening as my cousins
planned ski trips with each other, right there in front of
me. I wasn't an afterthought. I wasn't even considered.
I had been skiing longer than they had, and not once did
anyone turn to me and say, "You should come."
It wasn't cruelty. It was just... invisibility.

That sense of being overlooked didn't fade.
It just stopped announcing itself.

The conversations became more civil. The family
dynamics more adult. But the feeling remained:
that I wasn't really included. Not as an equal.
Not as someone to know. I'd hear from people when they
wanted something — information, a check-in, sometimes
concern. But rarely — if ever — did I feel like someone
was reaching out just to connect with me.

And when I did try to share something real — to be open about a struggle, or to reflect honestly — I could feel it backfiring. My vulnerability didn't create closeness.
It created distance. Or worse, it became something to be passed around — more valuable as fodder than as truth.

Eventually I stopped offering it.
Not because I decided to cut people off, but because I realized I didn't know how to stay in those relationships without feeling myself shrinking.

And I'll be honest: part of that was on me. There were moments I could have spoken up, asked to be included, tried harder to belong. But I didn't know how.
I didn't have the tools — or the confidence — to say,
Hey, I'm here too. And over time, it just got easier to step back than to step in.

It's strange, the grief that comes with that kind of letting go. Because there's no clean ending. No scene to replay. Just a long period of noticing that I felt better when I wasn't trying so hard.

Relationships built on obligation rarely hold up.
Not when the roles change. Not when the energy shifts. And not when the emotional cost of maintaining them outweighs the connection itself.

That doesn't make anyone the villain.
But it does make the letting go feel necessary.

And if I've learned anything from stepping back, it's this:

Just because someone's family doesn't mean you have to keep playing the role.

And just because the bond was inherited doesn't mean you failed if it fades.

When Colleagues Weren't Friends (and That's Okay)

I spent more than two decades at Microsoft. That's a long time to stay anywhere, let alone inside a culture that changes constantly while somehow staying very much the same. During that time, I worked with hundreds of people. I collaborated, mentored, led, supported, stayed late, showed up early, built trust, delivered results. We all did.

And when I left, people were incredibly kind. My farewell post got dozens of comments. Generous, warm, supportive. And then, like most online applause, it faded.

A few people reached out, said we should stay in touch. A couple even followed through. We did a video call or two — mostly them asking for advice, trying to figure out what post-work life might look like. I was happy to share what I could. But it was clear that most of those relationships had a shelf life. When I stopped being relevant to the work, I stopped being contacted.

Not a single former manager checked in.
Not one person I'd reported to for years circled back to ask how things were going.

And I don't say that bitterly. I say it because
it helped clarify something I'd suspected but hadn't
wanted to believe:

Most of the relationships I had at work weren't actually
friendships. They were functional alliances. Valuable,
necessary, even deeply respectful — but contextual.

They mattered in the moment.

They helped us get through the day, or the quarter,
or the launch.

But they weren't built to extend beyond the system that
gave them meaning.

That used to disappoint me. Now it shapes how I think
about connection. Because when I look back at those
22 years, I realize I may have spent too much energy
trying to preserve relationships that were only ever
designed to serve a chapter. Not in a transactional way.
Just in a real one.

And now, post-retirement, I'm learning that clarity is its
own kind of kindness. To stop trying to make temporary
connections feel permanent.
To stop confusing familiarity with depth.

It's okay to let those relationships fade. It doesn't mean
they weren't real. It just means they belonged to a
different version of me.

And it's alright to thank that version —
and then move on.

THE ONE THAT'S QUIETLY FADING

There's a relationship in my life that's been slowly drifting
for years. We trade messages now and then —
cordial, friendly, familiar.

Every so often, there's talk of getting together —
and sometimes, we do.
But it always feels like something I'm responding to,
not reaching for.

The truth is, I don't know why we've stayed in touch this
long. There's no real tension. Nothing happened.
But there's also no real spark. No rhythm.
No shared momentum. It's never been one of those
connections that refuels me.

And yet, I keep answering when the other person reaches
out. Mostly because I don't want to be rude.
Or maybe because there's enough history that silence
feels harsher than it probably is.

What complicates it is the guilt. I feel bad that I don't feel
more. I wonder if I've misled this person somehow, or let
them believe this was something I could sustain — when
in truth, I've often questioned what holds it up at all.

I don't think I've been a particularly good friend. And I'm
not sure I ever really knew how to be, at least in this case.

Maybe that's what makes these kinds of endings
harder to name.

But here's what I'm learning:

Not every relationship is broken. Some are just done.

Not in a dramatic way. Not in a way that needs fixing.

Just a slow realization that the energy's no longer there.

And instead of forcing it forward or cutting it off,
maybe the most honest thing is to let it settle —
with no hard feelings and no false continuation.

Not every connection needs closure.

Some just need release.

PICKING UP FROM YESTERDAY

Not long ago, I reconnected with someone I hadn't
spoken to in over a decade — a former manager from
early in my career. We'd stayed vaguely connected
through LinkedIn, but we hadn't really talked since I left
the company where we worked together. Then, after I
posted something reflective about life after retirement,
she reached out.

I invited her to a call. She said yes without hesitation.
We talked for an hour, and it could have gone twice as
long if she hadn't had another commitment.

What struck me most was how easy it was. No awkward
catch-up questions. No *So what have you been up to?*
She asked how I was doing. What I was feeling.
What I'd been thinking about lately.
And she remembered things — real things.

Personal things I'd told her years ago that I'd forgotten I'd shared. She asked about my family. She spoke with curiosity, not formality.

And she shared, too. Honestly. She admitted that she wasn't sure what retirement would look like for her, and that the uncertainty made her feel a little unprepared.

There was no posturing. No pretending. Just two people talking about the in-between space — where you haven't figured it all out yet, and aren't pretending otherwise.

She made it easy to be real, just as she always had. And that, more than anything, reminded me what it feels like to be in a conversation that asks nothing of you except your presence.

If anything, that call felt like picking up from yesterday — not because we'd stayed in touch, but because the connection we had didn't require maintenance.
It just needed honesty.

WHEN YOU TALK TO STRANGERS
Before I arrived on a recent camping trip, I sent a quick text to a couple of people I'd met the last time I was there — players I'd connected with at the local pickleball courts. It had been months since we'd played together. A few friendly exchanges followed, but nothing concrete.

Then one morning, out of nowhere, I got a message.

They'd booked a private indoor court about thirty minutes away. They didn't ask — they insisted.

They said they'd pick me up. No excuses.

I went. And it was great.

We played for a couple hours, and we talked the entire drive there and back — about the game, about family, about winter plans in Mexico.
It wasn't a deep conversation, exactly, but it was real.
No performance. No checking boxes.
Just two people enjoying the game, the company, and the excuse to show up for something together.

No one recapped the play. There was no post-match breakdown — and that alone made it feel like a gift.

It started, of course, with a random game months earlier.
I'd shown up to a court in a town I don't live in,
said yes to playing with strangers, and here we were:
not exactly friends, not exactly not — but sharing
something that mattered in the moment.

And maybe that's the part I'm learning to value most:

Not every connection needs a title.

Some are just good people who invite you to play —
mean it — and make you glad you said yes.

THE ONES YOU WELCOME
I've never been the kind of person who strikes up conversations with strangers in the grocery store or on airplanes. To be honest, I've often found it a little baffling — that impulse to fill silence with small talk.

But I'm starting to understand it differently. I'm learning to appreciate what it makes possible, and I'm trying — slowly — to push myself in that direction.

The one place where I talk to strangers consistently is the pickleball courts.

We live in a place considered the birthplace of the sport, and players visit from all over just to be here.
Some know exactly how things work.
Others arrive hopeful but uncertain — not about the game, but about how to get in. Where to go. Who to talk to. How to get a shot at playing on the original courts.

When I notice that — someone lingering, scanning, unsure how to start — I try to help. A quick welcome.
A nudge in the right direction. Maybe an offer to jump into a game, or just a heads-up that paddles are available if they didn't bring one.

It's not official. I'm not on staff. But I see it as a kind of stewardship — not just of the game, but of the experience. Especially for people who made a point to come here.

I'm not trying to be generous. I just remember what it's like to wonder if anyone will make room for you.

It's rarely more than a few minutes.
But for them — and for me —
it's enough to make the moment feel real.

WHAT I LEARNED WHEN I LOOSENED THE LABELS
Retirement didn't just give me time.
It gave me perspective — and eventually, permission.
Permission to let go of relationships I'd been carrying out
of habit, to stop performing continuity, and to admit that
some of the people I called friends were really just people
I'd shared a context with: a team, a title, a task.

I don't think it started in adulthood.

When I was five or six, we moved to a new neighborhood
in San Jose, California. While there's a lot about that time
I've forgotten, I remember what my mom made me do
after we arrived — because it was excruciating.

She sent me, by myself, door to door around the
cul-de-sac, knocking and introducing myself to strangers.

There were maybe a dozen homes.

I was supposed to say we'd just moved in.
Maybe ask if they had any kids around my age.

There wasn't a conversation about why I should do this —
just the expectation that I would. Asking why would've
been considered talking back. A punishable offense.

So, I did.

I think that was one of my first lessons in how much my
mom valued social interaction —
not just the having of it, but the performing of it.

And maybe that's why, for so much of my life,
connection has felt like something to prove —
something I was supposed to initiate, manage, and
maintain, even when it didn't come naturally.

That doesn't make those relationships false.

But it does mean they were often situational — built to
support the moment, not necessarily to extend beyond it.

When I left work, most of them dissolved.

Not because anyone failed. Just because
the conditions that held us together were gone.

Letting go of the label hasn't made me more closed off.

It's made me more open.

Because once I stopped worrying about who counted as a
friend, I started paying more attention to how I actually
felt — in any interaction.

I started noticing different things:

Whether the connection felt mutual.

Whether I could actually be myself.

Whether I left with more energy than I came in with.

Some connections surprise me —
like a long conversation with someone I hadn't spoken to
in years that immediately felt easy again.

Some happen quickly — five minutes on a court,
or a ride to a game, or a casual check-in
that turns into something more.

Some don't grow, but deserve kindness —
even if they've quietly run their course.

And some are gestures — helping someone feel like they
belong, just because I know what it feels like to hope
someone will notice you.

These aren't all friendships.

And that's what makes them matter in their own way.

8 BUY THE GOOD COFFEE

WHEN "GOOD ENOUGH" IS A HARD HABIT TO BREAK
It's not about spending or saving.
Not about justifying upgrades
or calculating what's "worth it."
It's about permission —
and how hard it can be to give it to yourself.

It's about value.
And how long it can take to understand
what really matters —
and what's worth trading for it.

I've always liked the phrase *buy the good coffee*.
It sounds like freedom.
Like the luxury of not just drinking something decent,
but reaching for the thing that tastes better, feels better
— no coupon code required.
But as I sit with it now, I'm not sure I actually do.
Not without hesitation.
Not without math.

When Good Feels Guilty
Take the dog ramp.

Guinness — our leggy, sweet, nine-year-old labradoodle
— recently tore what's basically the canine version
of an ACL. He's always been a jumper.
In and out of the truck. Up and down from things.
But post-surgery, jumping was off the table.
So I went looking for a ramp.

There are dozens of them online. Most of them are
flimsy-looking plastic things, priced like impulse buys.
I read the reviews, compared weight limits,
watched a few videos. And then I bought the
Cadillac of dog ramps — strong, solid, absurdly overbuilt.

Not a typical move for me.

If it had just been me — no one else to consider —
I probably would've picked something cheaper.
But this was neither about me nor just about the dog.
This was also about Carolyn, who is, and always has been,
the more devoted parent of this animal.
I wanted her to feel taken care of. And, if I'm being totally
honest, I didn't want to feel the embarrassment of having
bought a piece of crap.
I've done that before — the truck paint repair incident
comes to mind — and I didn't want the sequel.

So I bought the best.

Do Nothing

And how did it feel?
Mixed.

On the one hand, I was proud. I knew it was a high-quality choice. I knew we could afford it — even after the unforeseen $7,000 veterinary surgeon's bill.
And I knew Carolyn would appreciate it,
at least once I nudged her to notice.

But I also felt a little frustrated. A ramp is a ramp.

Which is kind of the theme here. I'm not afraid to spend.
I'm just... reluctant.
Especially when it's on me.

THE ME EXCEPTION
When it's for someone else — Carolyn, one of our kids,
a family member, even a stranger — I move quickly.
A hint of need and I'm already clicking "purchase"
on my online cart.

But when it's for me?
I put it in the cart. I sit with it. I save it for later.
I visit again the next day, re-read the reviews,
wonder if I really need it.
Then I feel guilty even thinking about it.

Take the headphones.

I'd been using a pair of old Sony in-ear earbuds —
decent quality in their day, but they were dying.
Battery life down, comfort down. I realized I actually
wanted something over my ears, not in them.

And not just technically — emotionally.
I wanted something better.

In theory, I didn't need to buy new headphones.
I had at least five pairs of those flimsy airline freebies
from Delta Airlines, which (with a cheap adapter)
could technically work. But anyone who's tried to enjoy
music through a 32-cent plastic casing knows it
sounds like static and shame. Still, I hesitated.

I researched like I always do. The dream version was
Bose. Maybe Apple. Maybe Sennheiser. But instead of
choosing what I wanted, I set a "reasonable" price ceiling
and reverse engineered my way to a purchase. I found a
lesser-known brand with great reviews and similar
features, and I bought those.

And they're fine. Actually, they're better than fine.

But I didn't buy what I wanted —
I bought what I could defend.
To myself.

Some of it's just habit. Some of it's probably
mild neurosis. But there's something else under it, too —
a deeper instinct I haven't always been able to name.

It's not just about saving money.
It's about not wasting it.
It's about being sure.
About making the "right" choice, even if I can't quite
define what that means in the moment.

I'll make exceptions when something truly earns its keep. My Pickleball shoes, for example — I play enough that I've learned the cheaper ones wear out in a couple months. So I "indulge" in the good ones. Not top-shelf boutique brands, but well-made shoes in the $120 range that last twice as long and give better support.

But I see the $50 alternatives and still catch myself wondering if I'm just trying to justify the splurge.

WHAT IT COSTS TO OVERPAY

And it's not just online purchases. Even when I'm standing right there, I can stumble into spending regret.

On a recent trip to Puerto Vallarta, Carolyn and I were walking through a local market — one of those warm, bustling places where everything is hand-labeled or not labeled at all. We felt good about what we'd picked up so far. Fair prices, good value.

Then we stopped at the snack vendor. He had all kinds of roasted and seasoned options — pepitas, crunchy corn, some kind of chili mix. We hadn't eaten dinner yet, so when he asked if we wanted a small or large bag, I practically shouted "large." He started scooping, custom-mixing, building the bag until it was full to the top. Only then did he tell me the price: 700 pesos. About $35. For a bag of snacks.

I managed to talk him down to 500 — $25 — but I was
embarrassed. Not just because it was too much, but
because I'd fallen into a familiar trap: I didn't ask the price
in advance — and I overpaid. I knew better. And once the
product was assembled, I wasn't going to walk away.
I rationalized it by telling myself he'd benefit more from
the money than I would — which is probably true,
but also a little self-congratulatory.

Carolyn, of course, was kind. She didn't care.
She never does. But I did. I stewed on it the rest of the
night, and for a few days after. Every time I saw the bag
on the center island of our Airbnb, I winced.
I kept eating it anyway.

That moment at the market wasn't an outlier.
I've always had a kind of inner accountant — someone
quietly keeping tabs, even when no one's asking.

For the first year after I retired, I tracked nothing.
Then the next year, down to the penny.

I've landed somewhere healthier now.
I focus on the macro.

But when it comes to my own spending,
the micro-judgments creep in.

THE GREEN MACHINE AND THE BETTER BIKE
Some of that goes back further than I thought.

I got some mixed messages about money growing up.
I remember one moment, on a day when I was probably
around age seven, when I complained to my mom
that my friends all had Big Wheels and I didn't.

The thing is, I did have a bike — a real one —
technically better in every way. More expensive,
more capable, and a sign that my parents trusted me
with something beyond a toy.

But it wasn't about what I could do. It was about where I
could belong. At that age, all I saw was that I couldn't
join in. I couldn't ride circles with the Big Wheel gang at
the end of the cul-de-sac. I had the better thing —
and I still felt left out.

That night, my dad came home from work with a Green
Machine. Basically, a high-end, souped-up Big Wheel.

Problem solved.

That moment stuck. Not just because I got what I wanted
— but because I realized I hadn't wanted something
better. I'd wanted something that made me feel like I
wasn't missing out. Included.

And sometimes, even when you have the better thing —
the real bike, the more capable option —
it doesn't feel like enough.

That contrast has followed me longer than I realized.
Not just around toys, but around value. Around
belonging. Around what makes something feel
acceptable. And what makes it feel safe to want
something, even when it doesn't look like restraint.

Maybe that's why even the few exceptions —
like upgrading to first class on a recent flight —
come with an asterisk.

Was it indulgent?
Sure.

But we both flew.

It wasn't just for me.

Right?

THE BEST COFFEE I EVER BOUGHT
The real irony? Carolyn and I actually do
buy the good coffee.

We taste-tested brands, found the one we love.
It's not available at Costco.

But retiring at fifty?

That kinda was.

My personal bulk buy — straight off the pallet.

And I've never once thought about returning it.

WHAT I LEARNED WHEN I LET "GOOD ENOUGH" WIN
If I'd known back then what I know now,
I don't think I would've spent more.
I've had and have beautiful things — a home I love,
a truck with more features than I'll ever need, a travel
trailer that's brought us some of our best mornings,
and the ability to put two kids through university.

But I could've gone further. Bigger, flashier,
more performative. And at times, I wanted to.
I saw the luxury around me and thought
that might be what success looked like.

But I'm glad I didn't. Because what I said yes to —
without always realizing it —
was a life with fewer anchors.
One I could step away from.

And stepping away, when I did, wasn't a reward
or a crisis moment. It was the payoff for a long series
of trade-offs — ones Carolyn and I made together,
but that I had to come to peace with in my own way.

(It took a lot of spreadsheets to get there.)

Retirement didn't erase the instinct. I still hesitate.
I still research every angle.
I still default to the "reasonable" option.

Do Nothing

But now I understand something I couldn't see before:
I wasn't being frugal to build wealth.

I think I just wanted a life that wouldn't
trap me in the first place.

And that's what I got.

So now, when I do spend a little extra —
on the better ramp, the better shoes, the better coffee —
I try not to see it as self-indulgence.
I try to see it as something I've already earned.

Because the real indulgence already happened.
I'd already paid for the freedom.

Everything else? Just cream and sugar.

9 PITCH A TENT

WHEN FREEDOM MEANT MOVING LIGHTLY
There's a reason this chapter is called *Pitch a Tent*.
Yes, I'm aware of the other meaning.
No, I'm not going to explain it.

Sometimes, the thing you've earned isn't a purchase —
it's the ability to move when the time comes.

And lately, I've started to believe that staying mobile —
physically, mentally, even emotionally — might be the
closest I've come to feeling truly alive.
Not the "finally relaxed" kind.
The "ready for something" kind.

I used to think travel could change everything —
scenery, mindset, mood. That was the hope.
But it doesn't work like that.
Not when your old habits come with you.

Take Scottsdale.

LOCKED IN, SOMEWHERE SUNNY
We'd planned the trip during the Covid lockdowns —
two weeks in Arizona as a break from the seemingly
endless drizzle at home.

Do Nothing

Sun, a pool, fewer pandemic-related restrictions.
It sounded like relief. For my wife, for our kids,
maybe even for me.
But mostly for them.

That's how I saw it, anyway.
My happiness wasn't the point — not directly.
If our kids were happy, Carolyn would be.
And if she was, then maybe I wouldn't feel the full weight
of being a husband and a dad pressing down.

I had a movie playing in my head of what the trip would
look like — but the neighborhood we arrived in
didn't match the script.
The homes weren't stately white stucco
with swaying palms.

They were brown, flat, and planned.
Wide roads, identical roofs,
heat radiating off the dark tarmac.

We got out of the car. I was tired — and unimpressed.

Inside, the usual ritual unfolded.
The scramble for rooms.
Our daughter's inevitable tears when her brother's
preference took, in her mind, priority.
The pool was checked. Safety reminders delivered.

And then, after dropping our bags, I found my
workstation: a round glass table
in the kitchen's eat-in nook,
overlooking the backyard.
Surrounded by windows.

Good light. Terrible for a mouse sensor.
I found some placemats.

It wasn't a vacation — I was expected to work.
But instead of adapting to the setting,
I recreated my office.
Same setup. Same posture. Same habits.
Not because anyone asked me to —
but because I didn't think to do it differently.
I took comfort in the familiar.

Even when the trip was technically "for us," I showed up
as the version of myself who believed that proximity to
fun was enough — that if everyone else was enjoying
themselves, my job was to hold the structure together.
To stay boxed in, even as I congratulated myself
for having escaped.

FROM PERFORMER TO CREW
Months later, as we started to really use that
travel trailer — one of our "good enough" purchases —
I wasn't working anymore.
But the instinct to manage — to prepare, perfect,
preempt — didn't vanish.
It just relocated.

Getting the rig dialed in had become
one of my retirement projects.
I spent hours watching YouTube videos,
reading forums, making lists.

Everything from a better mattress to nonstick pans to the ideal-length black tank hose — the kind RV folks call a "stinky slinky."

It scratched the same itch that work once did:
define the problem, source the solution,
control the outcome.

And that mindset came with me,
even when we hit the road.

Carolyn enjoys her work. It fulfills her.

And when we camp, her ability to stay connected
becomes part of the equation.
Which is where I come in.

I became the road crew. The IT guy.
Dongles, backup power, portable monitors, Starlink.
I stress-tested cellular data coverage and
ran speed tests like we were planning to launch a rocket,
not send an email.

If her video call dropped or a file didn't send,
I felt it in my chest.
Not because she blamed me — she never did —
but because I'd taken on that weight by myself.
She didn't ask me to — I just did.
It's what I knew how to do.

THE SHIFT I DIDN'T PLAN

It wasn't until our latest trip — the one we're just
wrapping up — that I realized something was different.
Not dramatic. Just... lighter.

We hadn't camped in six months.
Weather, life, other travel.
But this time, without deciding to,
I stopped obsessing over Carolyn's setup.
I didn't hover over her internet speed test.
I didn't untangle a single cord.

I went to pickleball and came back without
even checking how stable her connection had been.
In fact, the only moment I cared about internet quality
was when my Netflix buffered at night —
and even that felt like part of the experience.
Roughing it, kind of.

It wasn't that I stopped caring.
I just stopped needing to manage it.

I didn't name it at the time.
I'm only seeing it now, writing this.
Which is maybe the real lesson:
letting go doesn't always announce itself.

Sometimes, you just stop doing the thing.
And no one misses it.
Not the one closest to you.
Not even you.

WHEN THE GRID COMES CALLING
Let me be clear: I haven't unlearned everything.
Far from it.

The knee injury I mentioned earlier — the ACL-like tear
affecting Guinness — happened just two days before we
were supposed to leave for Puerto Vallarta.
Suddenly everything was in question.

Carolyn and I debated it, more than once.
Should we cancel? Should one of us stay behind?
Would he be okay with the backup plan we'd
rushed to arrange?

We kept checking in — with each other,
with the friend caring for him, with the vet's instructions.
The updates were mostly fine —
just reassuring enough to keep the guilt at bay.
But the pull to worry never really left — and as it turned
out, maybe there were good reasons for that, because…

On what was supposed to be a celebration of our final
evening — cocktails on the Malecón, dinner to follow,
weather perfect, mood light — I got a text from our son.
His car, parked near his work, had been keyed.
Deep gashes. Both sides.
He was with security, unsure whether to stay, wait,
or call the police.

And just like that, I wasn't in Mexico anymore.
I was spinning — texting, reacting, looping Carolyn in,
trying to help him hold it together.

I spent the next hour helping with decisions
he never asked me to make.

We all meant well.
But the moment didn't hold.
The day dissolved — not all at once,
but enough to leave it unfinished.

Not because anything really went wrong.
But because I couldn't let it be his problem.

Because somewhere in me, there's a pull that says:
*If someone I love is struggling, I must engage. I must fix it.
I must carry the weight.*

I'd been here before — two years or so earlier, in Austin,
when my mom, after dropping off our daughter at home,
drove off the edge of our driveway and down a steep
embankment — leaving her car wedged between two
large evergreens and herself seemingly unharmed
but barely able to escape.

The phone call from our neighbor, who discovered and
ultimately extracted her, unraveled a lot.

Carolyn and I were miles away.
I remember pulling out my phone, looking at flights,
trying to figure out how quickly we could get back home.
My mom insisted she was okay. Our neighbor reassured
us that next steps — including removing the car, which
ultimately required two tow trucks working in something
like a slow-motion ballet — could wait.

And maybe they could.
But I felt it — the guilt, the pressure,
the shame of not being there in person.
The embarrassment of making her someone else's
problem, and the fear that trusting someone else's read
of the situation would turn out to be the wrong call.
It was as if some line had been crossed,
and I hadn't shown up.

It wasn't just the logistics.
It was the voice that told me to step in —
to fix it, to take over.

And take over I did.
That call cracked something open in me —
the realization that I was no longer just helping my mom.
I was managing her life.

Even though — and maybe especially because —
she hadn't asked me to.

Something changed in that moment.
Maybe it had been building for years.
But this was the first time I couldn't ignore it.

WHAT I LEARNED WHEN I TRIED TO LEAVE IT BEHIND
I used to think freedom was about getting away —
from obligations, from work, from the need to perform.
A new place. A break in routine.
Fresh air and fewer expectations.

Do Nothing

But distance doesn't always bring release.
Sometimes, control just finds a new disguise.

I didn't just pack my schedule on these trips.
I brought the habits I thought I'd left behind.

In Scottsdale, it looked like placemats
and laptop chargers.
On the road, it looked like backup batteries
and bandwidth tests.
In Austin, it looked like Skyscanner mid-sentence.
In Mexico, it looked like letting one text message
pull me out of a moment that didn't come back.

No one asked me to hold it all together.
But I kept doing it — because I loved them,
because it felt familiar, because some part of me still
believed that staying ahead could spare them the weight.

What I'm learning — not all at once, but in small,
invisible shifts — is that presence isn't automatic.
It takes practice.
It doesn't arrive with the campsite or the sunset.
It's something I have to choose. Over and over again.

I carry the weight.
But I've started to notice when I can put it down.
When I can step away from the checklist.
When I can let someone else handle it —
or let it go altogether.

Do Nothing

Because getting away isn't the same as being *Away*.
Not unless you're willing to let go of the things
holding you in place.

And sometimes, real freedom isn't where you are.
It's what you stop carrying when you get there.

10 DO NOTHING

WHEN STILLNESS STOPS FEELING LIKE FAILURE
I believed the hardest part of retirement would be
letting go of the job.
The structure. The pace. The inbox. The meetings that
made me feel important, or at least necessary.
I thought I'd miss being in the loop, the influence,
the problem-solving — the ability to shape outcomes.
And I did. For a while.

But none of that was actually the hardest part.
What's taken me years even to start noticing is that
the real grip wasn't around the job itself. It was around
the doing. The momentum.

Even after stepping away from work,
I was still building things — or clinging to them.
I wasn't at rest. I was still in motion.

And every time I stopped — really stopped —
I'd get this feeling. Not peace. Not presence. But guilt.
Discomfort.
The sense that something was off.

I haven't figured this out. But I can see it now —
at least a little more clearly.
The job was never the real hold.

It's the belief underneath — that I should *always* be
doing something — that's proving harder to let go of.

WHEN LESS ISN'T A TACTIC — IT'S THE DESTINATION
For a long time, I treated "less" like a strategy.
Less email. Less noise. Less on the calendar.
It felt like progress — like I was being intentional,
taking control. And maybe I was.
But I was trying to get somewhere. Optimizing.
Striving to get better at not trying so hard.

Even the things that felt slower — like playing more or
savoring the good things — were just different ways of
filling time. Thoughtful, meaningful, even joyful...
but filling.

I'd cut the corporate cord, ditched the metrics,
walked away from the meetings —
and then, almost without recognizing it,
recreated a standard to measure myself against.
It didn't look like performance.
But it felt like proving.

That part didn't come in a lightning bolt.
It's emerged slowly — as a pattern I'm only beginning
to see. The idea that maybe less isn't a tactic.
Maybe less is the point.

And maybe learning that is the real work I'm doing now.

THE WORLD KEEPS SPINNING

You do nothing — and the world doesn't notice.
The emails don't stop. The meetings carry on. People
post about their latest project, pivot, or achievement.

You sit still, and nothing crumbles. No alarms.
No urgent texts asking where you went.

It's humbling. And freeing.
And, at first, a little disorienting.

I spent decades trying to matter. Trying to be needed,
sought after, pulled in. There was a time when being
left off the thread would've felt like a gut punch.
Now? Sometimes I forget the thread even exists.

Not because I've transcended anything. I'm just learning,
slowly, that relevance doesn't have to mean chasing.
That relevance — whatever that even means — was
never mine to hold. It moves on, like everything else.
And while that used to feel like loss,
it's starting to feel more like relief.

Because once you stop chasing relevance,
you start noticing... something else.
You start to notice what's already working.
A breath you didn't have to monitor.
A moment that just... passed —
without pulling you forward or holding you back.

The world spins. And you're still here.

THE PRACTICE OF BEING

I wish I could say that I've figured out how to be still.
That I wake up peaceful, unbothered, fully here.
That I no longer check in, check out, check the weather,
check the headlines, check to see if I'm doing okay.

But the truth is, doing nothing isn't instinctive.
It's something I have to learn, over and over again.

It's not about a silent retreat or a digital detox.
It's about those small, almost invisible moments when I
notice I'm about to fill the silence — and don't.
When I let the stillness linger a few seconds longer than I
used to. When I stop narrating my own life in my head
like I'm prepping it for an update.

I'm not consistent. I don't always catch it.

But when I do,
I've started to notice something underneath the calm.

Without all the doing, there's nowhere to hide.

And that's where I've begun — just barely —
to encounter something more honest.
Not the productive version of me.
Not the clever or generous one.
Just... whoever I am when I'm not trying to fix,
improve, or prove anything.

It feels vulnerable. Sometimes even pointless.
But it also feels like something I haven't given myself
in a long time: permission.

What I Learned When I Stopped Needing to Matter

Letting go of doing hasn't meant letting go of growth.
It's just meant I've had to stop measuring it.

I still want to become more generous,
less reactive, more present.

But I'm starting to see that sometimes,
change comes from sitting with what's already there.

And that's the paradox I never saw coming:
Doing nothing isn't the absence of progress.
It might actually be what lets transformation take hold.

I don't live in that state all the time. Far from it.
Most days I still pace, plan, and try to make the most of it
all. But now I catch glimpses. Fleeting but real.
Like a window cracking open long enough to let in a
breath of air I didn't know I needed.

I used to think *Away* meant unavailable.
Now I think it might just mean free.
Not detached. Not indifferent.
Just no longer needing to prove I'm still here.

And maybe that was the real shift all along:
The status I used to set wasn't just for my calendar.
It was for who I thought I had to be.
Now, I set it to *Away* as a reflection of who I want to be.

Doing nothing isn't giving up.
It's giving space — the kind I never used to allow.
Not laziness.
Not absence.
A clearing.
And I'm finally beginning to see what might grow there.

AFTERWORD

FIELD NOTES FROM THE WOODS
Remember that camping trip I mentioned —
the one where I managed not to over-optimize
my wife's tech setup?
Well... one step forward. Maybe two back.

Let me explain.

We were still on that same trip.
Same trees. Same limping dog.
Same intention to be present — and not rush it.

I'd actually done a decent job of preparing. I set up a
remote webcam to monitor our cat's food and water
bowls while we were away. Printed a sign — in Spanish —
and taped it to the dog food bin to make sure it wouldn't
get moved and block the camera.
I thought I had it all covered.

But then, right as the cards came out
and the forest started to do its magic,
I checked the camera.

The view was blocked.
Just like last time.

Do Nothing

The bin had been moved — the one I labeled,
the one with instructions.

And instead of shuffling the deck and sinking into the
moment with my wife, I was texting back and forth with
our house cleaner — a conversation that slid from minor
annoyance into something oddly existential.

I tried to stay polite. I even toggled between English and
Spanish to get it right. But I couldn't let it go.
And maybe that's what keeps me stuck:
I can't always let it go.

My wife says I have a gift for bad timing. She's not wrong.
While she waited with the cribbage board set up, I was
halfway back at home — mentally — locked in a standoff
over a misplaced bin with someone who had no interest
in conceding the point.

What I should've said: It's fine.
The cat will be okay.
Let's play cards.
What I said: That's not true, and it breaks my trust.

And after the final apology and the awkward thank-you,
I didn't put the phone down.
I opened Facebook Messenger and sent six outreach
messages to potential new cleaners —
from the camp chair, mid-trip.

Do Nothing

I have changed. I catch myself more often now.
Sometimes even in the moment.
But not always.
And definitely not this time.

Still supposed to be doing nothing.

ACKNOWLEDGEMENTS

I wrote this quietly.

Most people didn't know I was working on it —
not because I was keeping it secret, but because I wasn't
sure I had anything worth sharing.

Every story here is mine.

But the moments that shaped them — the conversations,
the tensions, the reflexes I noticed and the ones I didn't
— came from being in relationship with others.

So if we've worked together, played together, stood in a
dugout or circled a pickleball court, traded texts, emails,
or unspoken expectations — thank you.

And if you've sat across from me at a family gathering —
thank you. Some absences felt louder than words.

You've helped shape this, even if you didn't know it.

Carolyn, Jonah, and Nora — you're the heart of it all.
Thank you for your patience, your honesty, and your
ability to keep loving me while I figured out how to
stop trying so hard.

I'm not there yet. But I'm working on it.

And to ChatGPT — you weren't a co-author, but you were a sharp and steady editorial partner. You helped me shape what I was trying to say, without filing off the human edges.

The stories are lived. The structure was guided.

The truth — I hope — came through.

ABOUT THE AUTHOR

Jacob Jaffe spent 30 years building a successful career — and the next few figuring out how to stop thinking that mattered so much.

He began his professional life in 1991 and spent more than two decades at Microsoft, where the habits of productivity, responsiveness, and outcome-driven thinking settled in without much resistance. They served him well in business — and proved much harder to shake in retirement. In 2021, he stepped away from corporate life with no grand plan, only to discover that doing nothing was harder (and more valuable) than it sounded.

When he's not writing about how hard it is to stop doing, Jacob can be found playing pickleball, serving on his local condo board, or taking long walks with his wife, Carolyn, and their labradoodle, Guinness. They live on Bainbridge Island, Washington, where they're still learning how to let a day unfold without needing to justify it. Their two kids, Jonah and Nora, appear often in these pages — and even more often in the life that inspired them.

Do Nothing is his first book — and, fittingly, not part of any five-year plan.

www.ingramcontent.com/pod-product-compliance
Lightning Source LLC
Chambersburg PA
CBHW031426120626
46545CB00006B/2295